January's Child

The Birthday Month Book

by **Andrea Alban Gosline**

Illustrated by **Lisa Burnett Bossi**

SCHOLASTIC PRESS

New York

Text copyright © 2007 by Andrea Alban Gosline
Illustrations copyright © 2007 by Lisa Burnett Bossi

Library of Congress Cataloging-in-Publication Data available

ISBN-13: 978-0-439-67268-9
ISBN-10: 0-439-67268-6

10 9 8 7 6 5 4 3 2 1   07 08 09 10 11

Printed in Singapore 46
First edition, January 2007

The text type was set in Mrs. Eaves
The display type was set in Gill Sans Bold & Mrs. Eaves
The illustrations were done in acrylics on watercolor paper

Book design by Elizabeth B. Parisi and Lisa Burnett Bossi

FOR OUR HUSBANDS

Carl Gosline, warmhearted and good.

Adrian Bossi, generous as time is long.

~ AAG & LBB

**January's child** is vibrant as wind,

whispering dreams as the new year begins.

You whirl like the breeze through leaves of a tree.

You are lively and hopeful and eager and free.

I inspire. I listen. I breathe. I unfold.
I receive. I believe. I adore. I am bold.

February's child is patient and bright,

like a shimmering star on a beautiful night.

You dance with the dewdrops, you light up a lake,

and you shine like a gem for the friends you make.

I reflect.
I am silent.
I sparkle.
I praise.

I am peaceful. I notice. I dream. I amaze.

March's child is true as the sea,

sailing to shore in the tide's harmony.

You are graceful and loyal, and playful and brave,

like the morning sun catching a blue-jewel wave.

I am constant. I journey. I touch. I am time.
I linger. I glimmer. I shimmer. I chime.

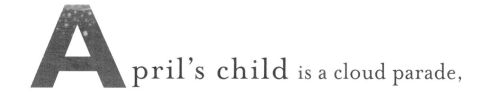**A**pril's child is a cloud parade,

where butterflies glide through the sky in shade.

You color the world the way you live.

You are curious, unique, and imaginative.

**M**ay's child is merry, amusing, and free,

gathering love like a large family.

You are happy as spring in a meadow row,

bringing your light wherever you go.

I bloom. I am grateful. I gather. I grow.
I turn. I am wondrous. I whistle. I sow.

June's child is caring, warmhearted, and good,

as the summer sky greeting her new neighborhood.

You are tender, and treasure small, feathered friends.

On this boundless love, the whole world depends.

July's child is the one who wills

to rise to the top of faraway hills.

You are swift and steady as you climb,

like the prance of a favorite nursery rhyme.

I begin. I am brave. I am sturdy. I chance.

I ascend. I am vast. I am cheerful. I dance.

August's child is generous as time is long,

like the garden's harvest and the meadowlark's song.

You give our world your bright bouquets

of kindness, grace, and courteous ways.

I am ripe.
I blossom.
I keep.
I care.

I stay.
I show.
I frolic.
I share.

**S**eptember's child is a faithful friend,

like the shore that waits at the journey's end.

You are sure of yourself as you strive toward your goal.

You inspire us with your loyal soul.

I watch. I discover. I voice. I vow.

I challenge. I am blessed. I quest. I allow.

October's child is the one who will reach

for all the lessons that life can teach.

Like a forest providing shade from the sun,

you protect and respect everyone.

I circle. I wonder. I call. I belong.

I awaken. I wish. I stand. I am strong.

**N**ovember's child is like sprinkling rain,

watering down on a windowpane.

You're the voice of friendship, the song of the wild,

applauding the spirit in every child.

I am proud. I am noble. I cherish. I tend. I cleanse. I remember. I weave. I bend.

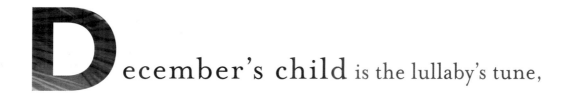

December's child is the lullaby's tune,

inspiring us to greet the full moon.

You question and listen, you know what is true,

and the light of the world accompanies you.

I am honest. I promise. I reveal. I learn.

I endure. I lead. I follow. I yearn.

You were born

in your very own month of the year,

and the world was waiting to welcome you here,

with daydreams and wishes and circles of love,

and, in turn, you brought a gift from above.